Mother Mourning

Mother Mourning

JOHN ZEDOLIK

RESOURCE *Publications* · Eugene, Oregon

MOTHER MOURNING

Resource Publications
An Imprint of Wipf and Stock Publishers
199 W. 8th Ave., Suite 3
Eugene, OR 97401

www.wipfandstock.com

PAPERBACK ISBN: 978-1-6667-6094-1
HARDCOVER ISBN: 978-1-6667-6095-8
EBOOK ISBN: 978-1-6667-6096-5

Table of Contents

Previously Published

"Ran Out" [with audio recording], in *TAB: The Journal of Poetry & Poetics*, Vol. 8.4, Chapman University, Orange, CA (July 2020)

"Sight Unseen," in *Today's American Catholic*, Hamden, CT (April 2020 issue)

"Specific Gravity," *Mystical Muse Online Poetry Magazine*, San Francisco, CA (August 2020 issue)

"Snowbird," in *Down in the Dirt*, Volume 179, Gurnee, IL (January 2021 issue)

"Heaven Knows," in *The River*, University of Maine at Farmington (April 16th, 2021)

"Once in Light," in *The Write Place at the Write Time* (Spring 2021)

"Wayfair," in *Today's American Catholic, A Journal of inquiry, reflection and opinion*, Hamden, CT (May 7th, 2021)

"Annual Sowing" and "Touched," in *Poets' Espresso Review*, Volume 14, Issue 2, Stockton, CA (Summer 2021)

1. The Days

Ran Out

Pork and sauerkraut feeds us
for days of dinner as no one

desires to cook upon return
from the ICU, as mother

has been crushed and lies
dying amid the tubes and machines—

so good luck to us as the tradition
insists, but I do not feel its force

as we finish the final leftovers
from the maker whose fortune

ended before I knew it, in this
new year auguring now hunger

for those of late so emptied.

Left

Breath of reptile

rattle and rasp

      Monstrous!

      Inhuman!

It is mother's last—

the shedding of mortal skin

the flicker-flicker-flicker
forked-tongue-gasp will pass,

will slither, softer, softer and die.

She is woman after all
and will be
spirit-breath with us

in us

slough off, slough off
the dross

only pure memory to glisten,
remain

Sunshine State

Gator keep gliding down
this warm and lazy river

you've got no concerns
for you've only cold blood

so couldn't care less about
my mother's consumption

by the quick-snapping jaws
of rolling rubber and steel

in its own stream though unlike
this one of glimmer and meander

through the subtropic scrub
and canopy whose shade we

must often seek even in this winter
light these reptiles must relish

as their eyes peep, sated, calm, above
the surface and its ripples, which

are all the teeth we need on this
sunny outing of still sharp grief.

Sight Unseen

The examination is annual
and routine, no haze or blearing

gleam: my eyes are clear
since the cataract surgery—

no churning Nile veil have they,
but mother's eyes have closed

this early year and will not open
again no matter the light,

and I will cry no crocodile
tears only the authentic gems.

*

The optometrist's drops
to dilate will only feed

the runnel that has worn
an unseen track, no foam

or splash. My pupils, dimes
and space-dark, will return

to own diameter and 20/20
designation, but the ducts

will drive down the water,
sight-obscuring seconds in the wash.

Then again the world will be clear
the only unseen, she who isn't here.

Specific Gravity

My tears wash the hard wood
of your box but cannot percolate

down to revivify your ashes
that lie sealed within, waiting

for a resurrection beyond
these footings and destinations

we take as home in our
limited ability and state

where the only alchemy
is to burn the body to this

square of mass heavier
than an equivalent order

of lead the ancients and medievals
would take as the starting

point in this process
on the road to gold

where my steps now are not
headed as I deposit that which

remains upon a gentle seat
that will ferry you to the end

lower than I can reach in my
capacity currently so weak

and laden with carved cedar
that pulls down, beyond root, down

To Rather Not

My secret sun is
the moon this second-month

night, weak orange and sliced
by the gossamer grace

of thin cloud like a poor blanket
lolling over the lowdown land,

arisen in the east, complement
to the western one's descent,

so my star now above the sleeping
blade of earth that I follow in stubborn

disproved belief, in defiance
of the day's end and certain

coming rise, so have deemed
this satellite my sun for the nonce, myself

companion to this wafered eye outshining
the stars whose light I cannot even see.

2. The Weeks

Industrial Strength

Memory stamps the new-woven
bolt of day:

>   mother has left this coil
>   and will not return.

A hard press, relentless pressure
and imprint to every thread dyed

new by the sun,

at rest over the third shift,
now pounding steel in the conscious

light upon which fabric
will wrap me for the rising

all the way until the repose in a gray garment
tailor-made for those remembering,

shadows in the folds that open

into empty

adamant as never again

My State

Dürer's *Melencholia* has
her polygon, putti, lamb,

and compass, among even more
paraphernalia to keep her occupied,

but I have only a drizzled veil
fading to life-lost bone-white

upon a canvas-land of bare
branches and plain

that stretches into the all
into which I must walk

unlike Albrecht's laureled
woman who just sits and gazes

with a disappointed eye
into the detailed distance,

whose lines and riches
I have not the luxury to imagine.

Acute Capability

I could slice a cold chunk
of the blue, as the ice-cutters

on northern lakes of old
but would only leave a cube

of dark to sag in hours
upon the surrounding hue

as air above is not water
below so not up to the burden

of bearing those weights
graver than lead or any

heavier metal upon a solid
surface, which is the sensible

method of support on this planet
cowed by physics, which I might

defy with my knife to the sky
and a sharp flourish and flash

to bring about the drop.

Notes to Last

1. Prelude: silence (for a bit)

2. Segue back to sound
    and all its accompaniment

   let it grow and flourish
   to eyes and ears

            movements: the span of years

3. Conclude with diminuendo
    to the silence once heard

and now the bulk of the piece begins

Consider the Lift

An old dog of indeterminate breed,
satisfied on the second-story porch
has made you smile in a time

when little inspires your face
to crease over teeth and even reveal.
Note that one element on this earth

has lifted you from the base of set
jaw and recent tears that keep one
pressing onto the ground.

The sentinel above has seen to that,
couchant in his comfort even if
unaware under his coat of light gold

of your soon and swift passage below
onto the next minute's block, your steps
yielding to the next, now not so very low.

Enforced Labor

Conventional wisdom calls
for pushing rather than pulling,

but I cannot get behind this sled
of grief that has harnessed me,

a draft-horse into enforced
service for an indeterminate

term of weight and effort
that bucks no slack or respite

but offers no stinging lash
beyond the first mile only

the dumb ton that threatens
to pull me under the runners

that would push me into the earth
into which I could not pull.

3. The Months

Memento

Ash Wednesday has marked
the faithful with a smear

of cross upon the forehead,
a smudge of grit to remind

the faithful of common end,
but mother is now wholly

burnt, exhausted to powder
in a fearsome flame.

That forging is the mark
upon me this Lent, as if burned

into me, body and spirit deep,
through my sinews and soul,

casting a sharp shadow upon
the earth, which will follow

me in this mindful season
and into the blooming next.

Once in Light

Her photo of the jacaranda's
upper branches may be a bit

overexposed, but the gist
of the subtropical burst—

reaching over the fence
into Avis's cracked back lot

like an insistent traveler
fired by fatigue and folderol

seeking his rented car of right model
after a long and hungry flight—

angled over from its roots
in the frontier of the retirement park

while the hibiscus down the pedestrian-only
land hides among the shade and lizards

without a photograph, which she will never
take in too-bright or otherwise Florida sun

as all has gone dark for her floral
zeal in all latitudes of blooming sense

into that non-apertured earth
whose focus is only set to forever.

Checked Progress

I turn to my mother's
ghost on occasion

to let her know
I am conscious

of her presence,
at which she smiles,

doubles her step,
catches up in her

short-sleeved blouse—
her purse at the shoulder

swinging but slowing,
stopping to return to its perch.

So certain now she is fit
to continue, I return my steps

to the route I have designed
but ready to check my steady

momentum with thoughts
of her progress ever behind.

Parting Gift

We watched the Game Show Network
after the rest had retired while my

mother was fighting for her life.
Charles Nelson Reilly was bantering

with Brett Somers, on *The Match Game*,
circa 1979, while host Gene Rayburn

(né Eugene Jeljenic)*

mediated the risqué laughs.

We were witnessing the phantoms
of those who had passed whom mom

would join in short days.

And after the badinage, a winner
arose near the time slot's limit

whose prize seemed paltry today
since passed is the value of much

that was once precious and desperately sought.

But she left forty years and then some

past the program, worth stable
even as she became naught.

*found in *Wikipedia*. Accessed 6 April 2020

Blank

Our last picture show illuminated
the night on November 29th,
the Saturday after Thanksgiving,

before the business of Monday
brought news of the theater's
closing and jettisoning of its

ticket-takers and popcorn-makers,
so fall crisped away, and winter
began to cling without any heat

of inspiration from the now-silent screen.
So sprung the new year, and the day
after, mother was struck by blind

wheels upon a rushing road,
and another scrim of silence
descended upon the scene,

now from spring to summer giving
battle to tiny death that blankets
the streets with a quiet of unseen

snow, another layer to peel,
another strata to dig, if full light
rather than a flicker returns to the frame.

Snowbird

I shoveled no snow in Pennsylvania
this past winter

but I did bury my mother in Florida
in the same season

so labored with a load heavier
than a shovelful

of snow no matter feather-powder
or weighty slush—

even in the welcome breeze
of seventy degrees,

the hibiscus flaring red-orange
upon surprised northern eyes,

palms waving easy greeting
in faux-summer skies

the mass returned to the earth
made more than muscles freeze.

Heaven Knows

Those blackberries at the bottom
of the neighborhood's hill above

the busway where I relished my
secret juicy treat beyond the diesel

exhaust must have migrated
to the stars like my mother,

who no longer rolls the *koláče*
and fills them with poppy seed

that only induced bliss instead
of narcotic sleep even though

I often consumed an entire roll
in a sitting after having been

mailed the boxed ambrosia
of the Carpathians through care and love

that is now lacking in my world like
the slope city-stripped, no doubt

by a dutiful public-works crew
just doing its job unlike

the driver and his wrong-way rush
in reverse toward the crushing

of my baker who will coax with skill
the sweet dough to rise no more.

Throne

My father at the end of his world
at the end of the road
near the creek

and the willow beside that creek,
in another's yard, which does not
weep as he does the months

without my mother, his wife,
which separate but may
engender solace as he

sits in the shade of his own
oak tree that offers relief
from the heat

of summer's heart that must
burn for him but in ice
that must freeze

in his hollows exempt from the effect
of sun and axis-tilt, caves, carved
mines at a constant cold,

an evening kingdom dim in the silent chill
of he who treads the ways of Nyx
under leaves in his plot alone.

Wayfair

The Viaticum swallowed us
in its bitter circumference

as she took her Last Rites
before leaving with her traveler's

portion for the higher road whose
surface now was fresh and smooth

while we forced down the gravel,
jagged chips, who were staying

below, the crust, acid, and gall
our only fare on that heaving day.

Magnetic Field

She could not have realized
upon pulling up the road
and out of the house's sight

that she would never see it
again or the leaves just turning,
as it was in the new days

of October, which still mimicked
or at least remembered the summer
just past that the thousand or so

miles south would never let go
so drawing down those inclined
to the endless heat, like a northern

dream, endless desire, but so real
in that line and landfall nearing
Cancer's fortunate cinch, so strong

and long-fingered, it would brook
her no return—only a flash of memory,
a glimpse—in its grip of final closure.

Sic et Non

She is translated to silence,
the language that lacks
all tongue

no Rosetta Stone to compare
known script and not,
just sealed voice

by any other name a void, no vibrating
vocal cords that might course
with vowel and consonants

arisen from concern and fertile mind,
now nothing but the indecipherable
she has left us all behind

Vbi Svnt?

Your ashes plummeting,
Hadrian *Imperator*, a gray veil
seeming to hang above

the Tiber while its breezes
plucked like starlings
at the grains

stripping the powder cloth
of a goodly portion
of its nap yet giving

the river god his sizable
due, to digest each bit
down to atom in its depths

to settle into the blind bottom
or cling to current ferrying
to the sea and further

dissipation. But my mother's
lie, discrete, in a boxed cube
within plastic and sealed

wood under the unmoving
earth upon which rain
and tears will tumble

to collect far from any
river so only seeping,
if not still, until vapor,

taken up by the cycle imperious
if only fair, the remains
untouched by weeping,

tighter than a mausoleum
in the Eternal City sacked
by Goths, sure and unappeased.

Non-Standard

Mother is—No—Mother is not.

       Mother was.

     Grammar must follow the fact

though my desire leads the verb's inflection astray

to a false depiction of the current situation

that better fits my wish for a present condition

      indicative of a living state.

Fallen

Mother rains upon
the early autumn earth,
gentle, three hours

since the middle
of the night, when
spirits drift down,

wind ruffling light
curtains, moistening
the thirsting dark

and its denizens
who rise to wonder
for seconds of need

then return to dreams
emboldened by the drops
to endeavors of silver

and shine from which
distills the liquor soothing
to the soul having lost

her in the flesh and bones,
who now scatters these soft
pearls that dissolve to bless.

Touched

I sleep under moon slivers
that seep through the imperfect

blinds so stripe my inner sight
with silver that must grant

sheen to dreams succeeding
my downfalling into sheets

that soften the shift from here
to never-is, nor was, and what-if,

strengthened by those slashes
to sword-keen and silk-slipping

so staying sharp to the break of rising
in those shades of another sun.

Proof Against

A great aunt's husband's
funeral was just a mass

and extended family gathering
with food for us unknowing

and liquor for the adults
who huddled in rings

of gray conversation
for a Sunday's slew

from morning to noon-pass
unaware of the young boredom

lingering at exclusive tables,
a side effect of the inoculation

the low number in years provided,
a needle's bite that now

we would be happy to feel.

Sure Sailor

Scuds the cardinal over the air
like a deft craft upon open water

well familiar after a hundred
pursuits of the goal that now

fits like a driving glove, soft leather
worn smooth in its most-used

spots, which recalls to me
the legend my father recounted

of that flash, bright wings
signaling the soul of the dear

departed and auguring all
will turn out well, so my tears

to turn vapor, their own spirit
commingling with mother's

now as she skims, dips
in her element across my path

more loaded but lightened
by that burst of life-red.

4. The Year

Annual Sowing

This year is new so free of the taint
of my mother's death but free also of her

presence whose mark was not
a stain but a bloom of violet, spray

of baby's breath upon the soil
of those warmer seasons

*

And soon will three hundred sixty-five
calendar days repeat and complete,

so cleansed of that crack running jagged
to eternal black

but blank of her summer blossom,
so cold winter white whose bones

as innocence afresh take, I must,
not knowing any better,

its spring shoot taken on trust

39

Bearing

I could carry you piggyback,
Mom, if the distance were too
far to make it home on your feet,

but you will never need the ride
(though fair recompense for your
toting me the term in womb),

for you are now light memory
whose weight rests on my soul
strong enough even with the lead

of grief to bear gladly the mass
whose earthward pressure only
spreads roots that splay down

to push up the stem, sepals,
petals that scatter love's pollen
I will breath in every remembering step.

5. Beyond

Close Examination

Under the bed lies the guitar mother
bought me, pale white flowers
of mold blossoming upon its shiny
back, ghosts less staying than her,
which I wipe away in easy swirls

of the wrist that remembers the contours
of the instrument to which I have not
pressed under my frame and articulations
for months more than twice twelve—
when she was still breathing here with us.

But I have resurrected the strings
and wood, exhumed them from the buried
box, to pluck and strum the remembered
chords, melodies, whose timber and tone
will always ring with her spirit's lasting notes.

The Circle

I.

Bowie's "Life on Mars?" plays in the dream,
on my old stereo, but I weep to think of my
mother's death in these times while three
older women, who could be the Fates,
aware of their deed, comfort me.

II.

Bowie's "Lady Grinning Soul" plays in my life,
on the old radio, as I turn it on and pick a few
bright notes on the guitar that still reposes
under the bed of past adolescent dreams
in the last minutes of my trip home.

III.

The worlds have closed the circle, the presaging
has met the present after a gap of months.
My experience is complete, and I
continue moving forward,
aligned but incomplete.

Single Use

Mother's eyes are ash
so she uses the moon's orb
when it is high, and strong

before the clouds' cold
custard—

as the Graeae did
the single, coveted peeper
in the privacy Perseus spoiled—

but my mother is a Grace,

and the only one, with no
need to bicker and grasp
among another greedy two,

who would only spoil the view
of my motion and rest below,
as I sleep under aegis of her glow.

Future Deposit

Your death forced up a volcano
of grief whose fire, ash, and lava
scorched all my island ground

but now cooled to hardened ridges
in the salve of soothing years,
which may bloom, fertile, as happens

with these erupted-up fields,
for which the end of you planted the seed
even as the source deposited the need.